"PARENTING BETWEEN CULTURES"

AFIUK CROSS CULTURAL PARENTING MANUAL

"WHEN YOU HAVE TO PARENT IN A CULTURE IN WHICH YOU WERE NOT PARENTED IN YOURSELF"

CROSS-CULTURAL PARENTING

SUPPORTED BY

COMMUNITY GRANT

BOMA : A Swahili word meaning "Homestead"

BOMA is our Cross-Cultural support and training that we offer migrant parents to help them and their children navigate the different social and cultural landscape of living in a Western (individualistic) culture. BOMA is for When you have to parent in a culture in which

COMPILED BY JACQUI GITAU

**CO-FOUNDING DIRECTOR
AFRICAN FAMILIES IN THE UK (AFIUK) CIC
(©), JACQUI GITAU, 2021**

AuthorHouse™ UK
1663 Liberty Drive
Bloomington, IN 47403 USA
www.authorhouse.co.uk
UK TFN: 0800 0148641 (Toll Free inside the UK)
UK Local: 02036 956322 (+44 20 3695 6322 from outside the UK)

Because of the dynamic nature of the Internet, any web addresses or links contained in this book may have changed since publication and may no longer be valid. The views expressed in this work are solely those of the author and do not necessarily reflect the views of the publisher, and the publisher hereby disclaims any responsibility for them.

This book is printed on acid-free paper.

ISBN: 979-8-8230-8371-3 (sc)
ISBN: 979-8-8230-8372-0 (e)

Print information available on the last page.

Published by AuthorHouse 07/25/2023

authorHOUSE®

Compiled by Jacqui Gitau
Co-Founding Director
AFiUK CIC
All rights Reserved; 2021
Oxford UK.
Only Trained Facilitators can use this material for training parents.

Registered Office: Regal Community Centre, Ridgefield Road, Oxford, OX4 3BY
Colchester Office; Winsley's House, High Street, CO1 1UG
www.afiuk.org ; Tel Tel: 07921 462949 / 07539455974

info@afiuk.org ; @AfricansinUK

CROSS-CULTURAL PARENTING CHALLENGES

Migration is about "getting a better life, and better opportunities for our children" and many parents take comfort in the knowledge that they are giving their children a great start in life despite the struggles of migration and /or leaving extended family behind.

Parents have so many hopes for their children, they might want them to become a doctor, engineer, or lawyer. They might want them to marry and have lots of grand-children. They undoubtedly want them to be happy.

However, many parents face many more challenges than they anticipated after migrating, and many struggle with the schooling system, and sometimes end up having to be assessed by social services for 'hurting or neglecting' their children. Despite being ambitious and enthusiastic for new beginnings after migration, many parents have found themselves being assessed by the Children's Social Services because of practices, beliefs, customs and cultures which conflict with the social norms and laws of the land.

Then, that dream starts to crack a little. Their children start acting 'British,' they may start dating British peers, they say they don't want to study medicine; they want to leave home to live with their friends; they want to become artists or musicians.

You may start to think: "This is not why we came to the UK!" But it's too late. You are now the parents of 'Third Culture children'. You are all part of a more diverse British society, and you may have to accept that your children are more integral to this society than from your country of origin.

AFiUK CIC have developed this parenting programme as a specific response to this situation of social conflict that many migrant parents find themselves in. Many parenting programmes exist which provide parents with information and strategies to improve family life, however this booklet is addressing the specific need of providing information and setting the social context of equipping parents to "Parent in a culture in which they were not parented in themselves".

These tools should help you to adapt your parenting styles as you get to understand a bit of the situation from your child's point of view; and that way you can all achieve a positive outcome in your family life.

These are some of the issues other migrant parents have wanted to address.

1) Finding a balance between your traditional culture and the British way of life.

2) Helping your children adapt to school in terms of their studies and day-to-day activities.

3) Helping your children make friends and deal with discrimination or bullies.

4) Dealing with children who want to wear clothes and go to places you don't approve of.

5) Dealing with children who want to date outside their ethnic group.

6) Ensuring your children don't become involved in violence or drugs.

7) Helping you to understand how to work with your child's school to ensure the best outcomes for your child.

The Aims of this training are to:-

1. Help you understand the main social differences between the culture of your new country and your country of origin

2. Help you to understand the legal and social framework governing child welfare and family relationships in the UK.

3. Help you to understand the Schooling system and how to have effective communication with your children's school(s).

4. Give you information on support agencies that exist to support you and your children in your local context.

To get the best outcome of this information, we suggest you join one of our parenting groups, or request for us to work with your individual family. Contact us on
www.afiuk.org

The Training is broken down in the following sessions:-

Session 1: Mentalisation,

- Assessment and Personal Evaluation of Parents' own life journey,

- learning to Develop Empathy for our children's feelings and needs.

Session 2: Understanding Child Development and Needs

- social and health needs,

- peer relations,

- parent-child relations

Session 3: Helping the child to develop self-confidence

- Ages and stages,

- Realistic and developmentally appropriate expectations,

- positive attention / praise

Session 4 : Improving children's self esteem

- Listening,

- communication and Praise

Session 5: Managing family through Family Meetings,

- House Rules,

- Appropriate Boundaries and

- Consequences for behavior.

Session 6: Parenting children and teenagers in a new culture

- Positive discipline,

- Assertive communication,

- Making choices

Session 7: Parenting in a Different Social and Educational Environment.

- Education pathways,

- How children learn,

- Home-school relations and

- Finding the best way to support your child's learning.

Session 8: Understanding different legal and social norms governing family life in the UK

- Safeguarding and Child Protection,

- Physical chastisement, Child Abuse,

- Harmful cultural practices such as FGM, witch branding, breast ironing, ….

Session 9: Part 2 of Understanding legal and social norms governing family life in the UK

- Domestic Abuse and Healthy Relationships

Session 10: Life Journeys and future pathways for parents and children.

- Positive community involvement,

- Improving Cultural Capital and

- Signposting to other agencies.

It is critical that we regularly reflect on our own lives as parents and carers. How are we experiencing life both for ourselves and as parents?

Use the triangle below to guide your reflection. Notice the traffic lights

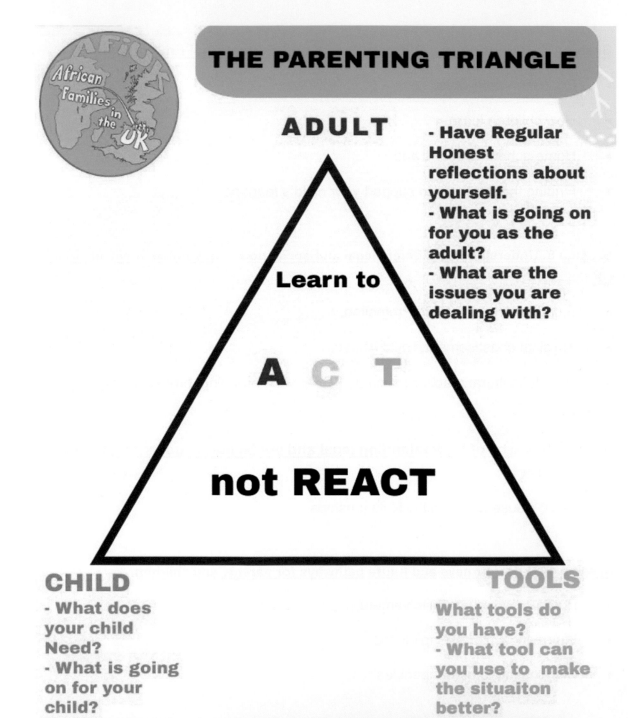

THE PARENTING TRIANGLE

ADULT

- Have Regular Honest reflections about yourself.
- What is going on for you as the adult?
- What are the issues you are dealing with?

Learn to

A C T

not REACT

CHILD
- What does your child Need?
- What is going on for your child?

TOOLS
What tools do you have?
- What tool can you use to make the situaiton better?

www/afiuk.org / info@afiuk.org / 07921 462949

Parenting in a new Cultural, Social and Educational Environment.

The basics of parenting such as love, nurture, support and encouraging our children are found around the world, but it is likely that you may have found the social behaviours, social systems and education system in the UK very different from your country of origin. And these differences will affect family relationships.

You may notice some of the following differences in as you adapt to family life in a new culture.

I Cultural Difference in the Society

Societies are usually classified as either *Collectivist (community-based)* or *Individualistic.* Collectivistic cultures emphasize the needs and goals of the group as a whole over the needs and desires of each individual. In such cultures, relationships with other members of the group and the networks between people play a central role in each person's identity. Cultures in Asia, Central America, South America, and Africa tend to be more collectivistic. Where collectivism stresses the importance of the community, individualism is focused on the rights and concerns of each person. Where unity and selflessness are valued traits in collectivist cultures, independence and personal identity are highly stressed in individualistic cultures.

For example, the UK is an individualistic society, where children are trained and encouraged to be independent as early as possible. Parents are expected to raise and support their children until they legally become an adult at 18 years of age. A British 16-year-old can have sex, learn how to drive a car and get a license when they turn 18, and at 18 they can leave school, get married, work full-time, and smoke, drink alcohol and vote. Many of them at this age often leave the family home to go to university, travel, or seek full-time work.

On the contrary, many communities from African and Asia are collective societies, where a lot of family roles and responsibilities are community-based. For example, in such communities a lot of emphasis is given to the role one plays in their community and children are trained and encouraged to consider the impact of their behavior on the wider community, and to consider respecting the norms of the community before their own interests.

You may find that you have to make adjustments in how you are parenting your child as they are growing up in an individualistic society when you yourself are from a collectivist society. This Parenting programme is an opportunity for you to learn strategies to help you get the best out of your family life as you discuss with other parents in a similar situation.

Illustrations by www.verywellmind.com

PERSONAL REFLECTION   ONE (I)

What are some of the main features of your community /	Which of these features are positive / What are the ad-	Which of these features are a problem? / Which disad-

You can continue on a separate sheet if necessary.

NOTES

_____

_____

_____

_____

_____

_____

_____

_____

_____

_____

_____

_____

_____

_____

_____

_____

_____

_____

_____

_____

II Family Life

Worldwide, family is important and valued as an important base for children to grow up safe and secure. Different communities have different roles for family members. In UK most fathers play a very active role in parenting; sharing equal responsibility with the mother and it is assumed that young adults will learn how to deal with financial matters and make personal and professional connections on their own, and even move out of home; this may be different in many community-based cultures where it is common for extended family members to live under one roof, and parents remain involved in their children's lives and decision making into young adulthood.

Along the same lines, UK children are taught to expect respect for themselves as individuals from a very early age. Spanking children is not tolerated, and many people think it should be illegal.

Positive parenting is based on mutual respect and treating your child as a person with equal rights to you. Parents are encouraged to listen to their children's thoughts and ideas, and negotiate, rather than give them orders.

This individualistic approach to raising children is reflected in later in life, when people are at school or in the workforce. Children in UK are trained to highlight their own accomplishments. This is a foreign concept in many cultures where people are encouraged to be humble, let their work speak for themselves and refuse compliments. Social culture influences how people behave, as well as how they view themselves.

Those in individualistic cultures might describe themselves in terms of personality traits and characteristics, e.g., "I am smart, funny, athletic, and kind." Those from collectivist cultures would more likely describe themselves in terms of their social relationships and roles, e.g., "I am a good son, brother, and friend."

PERSONAL REFLECTION   TWO (II)

How often do you speak to members of your extended family?

How many of them does your child know?

How well does your child know them?

Do you speak positively about your family identity?

Do you speak positively about your country of origin? Or do you use it as a threat when you don't like your child's behaviour?

Does your child know about your family tree?

NOTES

PERSONAL REFLECTION THREE (III)

*What are your thoughts about family life in this society? Use the columns below to write out what **hopes and what fears you have about parenting in the UK***

Hopes for raising my child(ren) in the UK	My Fears about raising my child(ren) in the UK

NOTES

_____

_____

_____

_____

_____

_____

_____

_____

_____

_____

_____

_____

_____

_____

_____

_____

_____

_____

_____

_____

III School System

There are also differences in the education system, including rules about school attendance and the statutory school age. The classroom culture is also different in how teachers relate to children in the classroom. In some societies, children may defer to the teacher and learn by quietly listening and gaining knowledge that way, while in the UK a lot of the learning is group work, and children are encouraged to be creative and critical thinkers and begin researching projects at a young age. In UK schooling children always move up each year, to which migrant parents may assume means that the children are doing well.

There is also a big expectation that parents will collaborate with the schools and engage more in their children's day to day learning. School and parents are partners each with equal responsibility for their child's education, and parents are expected to participate in the day to day learning of their children, much more than would have been expected say back in Africa. For instance, all children under 8 years must be accompanied by a responsible adult to and from school every day, and usually the child's teacher needs to see the adult that brought the child to school. This is most definitely a requirement of the early years' classes.

Parents can, and are encouraged to volunteer in their child's school, even classroom. Parents who have volunteered in this way report that they begin to understand the school system quicker.

The advantages of volunteering in your child's school are:-

⇒ you can observe your own child,

⇒ You can observe how teachers interact with students,

⇒ You can observe how children learn and how adults at school manage children's behaviour.

Many migrant parents have indicated that one of the key drivers for their family migration is so that *"our children can have a good education and a good future."* Engaging with your children's learning in this way will help you to achieve this goal.

Therefore to help your child's learning, we would encourage you to:-

⇒ Understand and work with the school system. Many schools will have a website, make a point of reading all the information and ask for help if you have any questions.

⇒ Volunteer and get involved in your child's school.

⇒ Talk to your child about school and their teachers in a positive manner.

PERSONAL REFLECTION FOUR (IV)

(Fill in these details about your child's learning if you have them. If you don't it is important that you get them as soon as possible as this is helpful to your child's learning)

What is the website of your child's school?

Do you have login details to your child's homework page?

Do you sign your child's homework diary?

When was the last time you read a book with your early years' child?

Or when was the last time your listened to your primary school age child reading a book?

Does your secondary school age child borrow books from the library?

Do you know if they read the books?

Does your family have membership of the local library?

When was the last time you went to the library with your children?

NOTES

_____

_____

_____

_____

_____

_____

_____

_____

_____

_____

_____

_____

_____

_____

_____

_____

_____

_____

_____
_____
_____
_____
_____
_____
_____
_____
_____
_____
_____
_____
_____
_____
_____
_____
_____
_____
_____

IV Family Relationships and State Intervention in Family Life

The common African proverb,

"It takes a whole village to raise a child";

may lead many parents to think that the responsibility to make all decisions about their child lies with them and their extended family or immediate community; whatever the circumstances.

In the UK independence, freedom of choice and equal rights for women are considered more important than cultural traditions. The law intervenes in family relationships and Domestic Abuse and cruelty to children are illegal. You can be prosecuted by law for emotional, psychological and physical cruelty to others, even if they are members of your family.

Remember that your children will be educated in British norms, have British friends, speak with a British accent, and be influenced by British and Western media. As part of a diverse British society, your culture and traditions will be respected if they are legal and healthy (we will discuss this more in the training).

Local Authorities or Councils are the local government in the UK. They are run by elected councillors, and cover a city, town, or county, and they are responsible for local services. County Councils are responsible for Social Services. They are separate from the national government and the National Health Service. Social Services employ social workers who are responsible for safeguarding the welfare of children in their area. Children's social services are part of the same directorate as schools and are separate from adult social services. They will usually be called Children's Services, or Children's and Family Services.

(You can read more about this here

https://www.childrenssociety.org.uk/sites/default/files/tcs/
rights_and_entitlements_card.pdf)

Although the idea of the government getting involved in how you care for your children may seem like a 'foreign idea', it is worth noting that

> Article 19 of the UN Convention on the Rights of the Child (1990),
>
> ". *"Children have the right to be protected from all forms of violence. They must be kept safe from harm. They must be given proper care by those looking after them*

Almost all countries of the world (and therefore their citizens) have signed agreement to this charter.

However in the UK, the government through the local Authorities have set up the law and polices to determine at what point a child's care and living conditions are likely to lead to the child suffering 'significant harm'. Should any concerns be raised regarding any child whether through the community, member of the public, the child themselves, school or health providers, the local Authority, through the Children's Social Services has a legal duty to make enquiries to assess what is happening to that child.

Although parents or carers may consider this assessment as an interference in their family life, Children's Social Services will consider this assessment to be in the "best interests of the child".

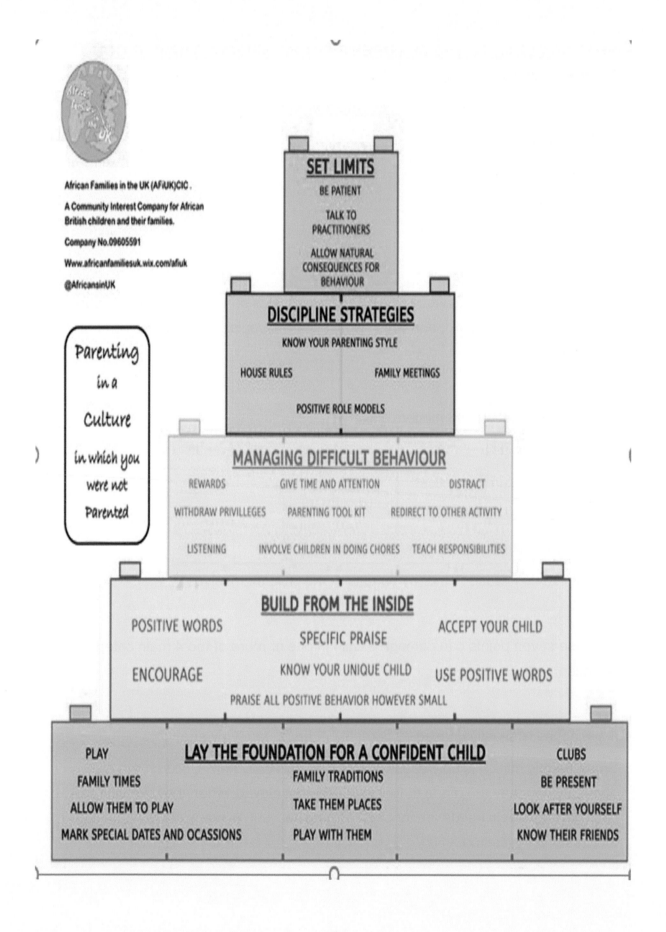

African Families in the UK (AFiUK)CIC .

A Community Interest Company for African British children and their families.

Company No.09605591

Www.africanfamiliesuk.wix.com/afiuk

@AfricansinUK

Parenting in a Culture in which you were not Parented

SET LIMITS

BE PATIENT

TALK TO PRACTITIONERS

ALLOW NATURAL CONSEQUENCES FOR BEHAVIOUR

DISCIPLINE STRATEGIES

KNOW YOUR PARENTING STYLE

HOUSE RULES   FAMILY MEETINGS

POSITIVE ROLE MODELS

MANAGING DIFFICULT BEHAVIOUR

REWARDS   GIVE TIME AND ATTENTION   DISTRACT

WITHDRAW PRIVILLEGES   PARENTING TOOL KIT   REDIRECT TO OTHER ACTIVITY

LISTENING   INVOLVE CHILDREN IN DOING CHORES   TEACH RESPONSIBILITIES

BUILD FROM THE INSIDE

POSITIVE WORDS   SPECIFIC PRAISE   ACCEPT YOUR CHILD

ENCOURAGE   KNOW YOUR UNIQUE CHILD   USE POSITIVE WORDS

PRAISE ALL POSITIVE BEHAVIOR HOWEVER SMALL

LAY THE FOUNDATION FOR A CONFIDENT CHILD

PLAY   FAMILY TRADITIONS   CLUBS

FAMILY TIMES   TAKE THEM PLACES   BE PRESENT

ALLOW THEM TO PLAY   PLAY WITH THEM   LOOK AFTER YOURSELF

MARK SPECIAL DATES AND OCASSIONS   KNOW THEIR FRIENDS

WHAT CAN LEAD TO THE CHILDREN'S SOCIAL SERVICES HAVING CONCERNS ABOUT A CHILD?

Child Abuse has been categorized into 4 areas

1. **Physical**

2. **Neglect**

3. **Emotional**

4. **Sexual**

There are also other situations which Local Authorities consider as likely to cause significant harm to a child, and which would warrant social services involvement. These are

1. Acute Bullying

2. Child exploitation and modern slavery

3. Domestic Abuse

4. Harmful (cultural) practices

5. Online safety

6. Radicalisation

7. Substance misuse (either by parents or the child themselves)

All these seven points can damage a child in one or more of the 4 main categories of abuse.

Child abuse is usually caused by parents or carers, rarely by strangers.

Some people think it is only abuse if a child is physically hurt. Children are also abused when they are made to feel worthless or unloved, when they live with violence or their basic needs are ignored. This leaves just as many scars and the effects can last a lifetime.

Child abuse and neglect is when a child is physically, emotionally or sexually harmed. It is also when the health, safety or wellbeing needs of a child are neglected.

Child abuse can happen in families of any income, culture or religion. It often happens over a long period of time. The effects of abuse and neglect are serious and can last a lifetime.

1. Physical Abuse

Physical abuse is when a child's body is harmed by things such as punching, hitting, shaking, biting or burning. There may be cuts, bruises or broken bones. Sometimes there are no signs because the injuries are internal. In extreme cases, children can die.

There are some cultural practices done to children's bodies, which hurt and maim them for life, such as FGM (Female Genital Mutilation, or circumcision, or breast ironing, force feeding.

Extreme punishment such as kneeling for a long time, carrying heavy objects beyond their physical capability and age, forcing to have cold shower in winter, rubbing chilli in eyes or genitalia

- Can you think of some of your cultural practices that are harmful to children?

2. Neglect

Neglect is the persistent failure to meet a child's needs.

A child's physical needs can also be neglected. They may not have a place to live, or live somewhere that isn't safe. They might not have enough food or clothes, or not be kept clean. They might be left alone or not be well supervised. Not supervising children while they are on the internet can also lead to emotional and sexual abuse, and it is neglect.

It is also neglect when a child is not given the health care they need, (when parents miss medical appointments), including mental health care, or when parents don't make sure the child gets an education – by missing school, or going late to school many times.

3. Emotional

Emotional abuse is just as harmful as physical abuse. It can be less obvious, so no-one might try to stop it. It is when a child is treated in ways that make them feel scared, worthless or alone. Children witnessing other people being abused – such as in domestic abuse, is also emotional abuse.

A parent might:

- ignore a child or refuse to accept them

- not show love, or withdraw love to control the child

- constantly shout at a child

- criticise, tease or shame them in front of others

- encourage a child to break the law.

- Cursing a child whether in anger, cultural or religious reasons.

Include here: Online Abuse, Lack of supervision while children using internet; as well as online grooming

4. **Sexual abuse**

Child sexual abuse is when an adult or older or bigger child persuades, tricks or forces a child into sexual activity. It includes sexual acts, inappropriate touching, showing the child pornography or involving them in prostitution. They may use threats or bribes to keep the child silent.

Children may be scared they will get into trouble if they tell, or that it will cause a lot of problems. They often feel no-one will believe them or that they are to blame.

While abuse by strangers does happen, most sexual abuse is by someone a child knows and trusts.

5.

> The cross-government definition of domestic violence and abuse is:
>
> *"Any incident or pattern of incidents of controlling, coercive, threatening behaviour, violence or abuse between those aged 16 or over who are, or have been, intimate partners or family members regardless of gender or sexuality.*

Domestic violence

We have included Domestic Abuse in this booklet because it is one of the most common problems facing families in the UK.

Living with violence harms children emotionally, even if they are not the direct victim. It affects their growing brain and can delay their development.

Children can feel they are to blame for the violence. They can feel powerless when a loved parent is mistreated, and ashamed that they can't stop it.

> **Controlling behaviour**
>
> Controlling behaviour is a range of acts designed to make a person subordinate and/or dependent by isolating them from sources of support, exploiting their resources and capacities for personal gain, depriving them of the means needed for independence, resistance and escape and regulating their everyday behaviour
>
> **Coercive behaviour**
>
> Coercive behaviour is an act or a pattern of acts of assault, threats, humiliation and intimidation or other abuse that is used to harm, punish, or frighten their victim.

Children can also be physically harmed when there is violence. They may get caught up in what's going on, or hurt as a way of 'getting at' the other parent. Children may be neglected because family life is so disrupted.

Children have a right to be safe and cared for in their own home.

The abuse can encompass, but is not limited to:

- Psychological

- Physical

- Sexual

- Financial

- Emotional

.

Source: https://www.gov.uk/guidance/domestic-violence-and-abuse - June 2018

Why Does Child Abuse Happen?

Not all parents mean to cause harm to their children. Some may be struggling with their own problems or might not know better ways to care for children.

Parents might:

- Find life hard and get very stressed. They might have problems with money, alcohol, drugs or their mental health. They might not have family support and lash out at their children when under pressure

- Not know how children learn and develop. They may expect too much from a child for their age and get angry when they can't do something

- Not understand their child's behaviour. A child needs to feel safe and secure but can't always say what they need or feel. A parent might think a child is being naughty when really, they are scared and need comfort. Children can also go back to younger behaviours when they are stressed, e.g. wetting the bed again when they have been dry.

Migrant parents have the additional strain of :

- loss of family support networks,

- dealing with racism for themselves and their children,

- economic hardship leading to long working hours,

- lack of knowledge of local family support policies and systems.

- Lack of stability and uncertainty about immigration status; this puts both financial pressure and stress on families, including domestic abuse

- Different practices, beliefs, customs and cultures of migrant families mean that many migrant children are put at risk of significant harm due to parenting practices and family life which is in conflict with UK family law.

Any custom or practice whether borne from culture or religion, is not an excuse to hurt or harm a child.

There are services that can help parents to look after their children well, even when they are under pressure.   AFiUK's main aim is to inform, train and support migrant families to adapt their parenting practices for best outcomes for their children, and to comply with UK family law.. At the first instance speak to your child's school, Health visitor or your GP.

Child abuse and discipline

Some parents hit children when they are angry with the child's behaviour. This can cross the line into child abuse. If you feel like hitting your child, it can help to ask yourself:

- Would it be OK for someone to do this to me?

- Am I taking things out on my child?

- If I hit my child, will they think it's OK to hit others?

Some parents have grown up with hitting and may not know other ways to teach children.

Hitting is not the best way to teach children. It teaches them that violence is OK. It is important they learn other ways to resolve problems. It is authoritarian, you may get the behavior you want in the short term, but your child will not develop to be an independent person who can regulate their own behavior.

They learn to fear you and may not learn the behaviour you want. Try to show children what you want, and then praise them when they do it. It takes time for children to learn. Be patient and remember to be a good role model as you are training disciples' .

The root of the word discipline is '**Disciple'**. A disciple is a follower of someone they believe in and who has modeled and passed on their values through training and positive relationship. To discipline is to **'Train for Life'**. The aim of positive discipline should be is to give your child life skills to be able to live fulfilled and productive lives. Aim for passing on knowledge and understanding, rather than instant compliance.

Effects of Abuse on children

When children are abused their trust in others is broken. This affects how they form relationships in the future. It can make them feel worthless, and they are more likely to develop low self-esteem and mental health problems.

They can be more likely to do risky things, e.g. using drugs and alcohol, having unsafe sex or breaking the law.

Abuse can change how a child's brain develops and how they learn. It can also make it harder for them to manage their feelings and behaviour.

As adults they can be at risk of getting into relationships where there is abuse. This repeats the cycle.

Break the cycle of abuse. Even if you don't see the effects of abuse straight away, the harm can go on for generations.

What you can do as a Parent

If you get upset and angry easily, there are services that can help you to manage these feelings. Don't be afraid to ask for help. Your GP or Health Visitor and Your Child's School / Nursery is a good place to start. You could also:

- Spend time with supportive, positive people

- Develop a network of family and friends you can talk to, and ask for help when you need it

- Seek help with the things that are stressing you in your life, e.g. money, relationships, drugs, alcohol

- Look after your health and wellbeing, including your mental health. With all the demands on parents, it can be hard to get the time to care for yourself. If you look after yourself, you can take better care of your children

- Learn about child development at different ages. You may be less upset if you know your child isn't yet able to do something you want them to do

- show your child what you expect of them calmly and patiently. Seek support if you need help with your child's behavior.

- Show your child that you love them in the things you do and say every day. It will help them to feel safe and secure.

- If there is violence in your family, it is important to seek help. It doesn't usually stop by itself.

- If you or your children are in immediate danger phone the police on 999

Child protection is everyone's business

Child abuse and neglect can be prevented or stopped. Everyone can help make sure children are safe.

In UK the Children's Protection Act seeks to protect children. It says that certain people must make a report if they suspect child abuse. This applies to doctors, nurses, dentists, psychologists, police, probation officers, social workers, teachers, family day carers, clergy and those working where services are provided to children, including sports.

The Children's Services and the Police have a legal responsibility to protect children. They investigate reports of child abuse and can remove children who are at serious risk.

People in the community can also report their concerns. It is important to do this even if you think it is not your business or you don't want to get involved. You could stop a child being harmed and help a family get support.

To read more about child abuse, what to do if you are worried about a child, and more details about the impact of abuse on children, visit the NSPCC (National Society for the Prevention of Cruelty to Children) website. (https://www.nspcc.org.uk/what-is-child-abuse/)

Authoritative parents encourage their children to be both assertive and self-controlled. Research shows that children of authoritative parents appear to be the best adjusted with good social skills. They are able to effectively regulate their emotions and impulses and are less likely to engage in problematic or antisocial behaviour. These children also have relatively high levels of self-esteem and happy dispositions.

From this research you can see that it is ok to be strong and to impart the positive values from your community, but allow your children some flexibility to discover themselves, while belonging to two different cultures. Nurture and encourage your children and guide them to determine their futures and shape their own beliefs, without the fear that you'll somehow stop loving or supporting them.

PARENTING STYLES

Researchers have identified four main parenting styles.

1.   The first style is referred to as **a permissive parenting style**. Permissive parents are warm and accepting, and avoid confrontation with their children. They make few demands of their children, allowing them to regulate their own behaviour as much as possible. Research suggests that children of permissive parents have difficulty regulating their emotions and controlling their impulses but have relatively high levels of self-esteem.

2.

2. The second parenting style is an **uninvolved or Neglectful parenting style**. Like permissive parents, uninvolved parents make few demands of their children. However, they show little warmth or responsiveness toward their children. Research shows that children of uninvolved parents tend to be the least well-adjusted.

3. The third parenting style is referred to as an **authoritarian parenting** style. Authoritarian parents provide highly structured and well-ordered environments for their children. They emphasize values such as respect for authority, respect for work, and respect for order and tradition. These parents expect their children to obey standards and rules and accept their decisions without question or argument. There may even be some physical hitting and other harsh punishment involved, which is not acceptable in UK. You could find yourself in legal trouble or your children may be subject to Child Protection by the Social Services, if you punish your children physically.

Research shows that children of authoritarian parents are usually more anxious and withdrawn than other children and tend to have relatively low levels of self-esteem and high levels of depression. However, these children are less likely to engage in problematic or antisocial behavior, and they tend to perform well in school.

4. The final style is an **authoritative parenting style**. Like authoritarian parents, authoritative parents expect their children to respect authority and provide them with explicit standards and rules of conduct. In contrast, though, authoritative parents prefer to reason or negotiate with their children when attempting to resolve conflict.

PERSONAL REFLECTION   FIVE (V)

What parenting style do you use (more)? Why?

What about your partner?

What are some of the things that you do as a parent that work well

What areas in your parenting practices do you think you need to change / adapt?

NOTES

High

Behavioural control; demandingness

Low

Authoritative

standards
enabling
flexible
supportive
Democratic
guidelines
assertive
Self-regulation
warmth, supportiveness

High

Permissive

no guidelines
lenient
indulgent
appeasred
Over-involved
You're
the Boss
blurred roles
Non-directive

Authoritarian

Punishment
Rigid
Because
I said so
Obedience
Status
Directive
Structure
autocratic
Rules
I'm the
Boss
responsiveness,

Uninvolved

uninterested
distance
passive
absent
neglectful

Low

self at the start of the programme? And then again at the end of the programme? Score yourself as per the chart below

*Family traditions – these are those you do as your family, not your tribe or your community

SELF EVALUATION ON PARENTING CAPACITY

0-2		I don't know what to do / I don't know what this means
3-4		I know I need help, and I am accepting help
5-6		Trying, but it's a struggle
7-8		We are comfortable / confident about this
9-10		We are completely fine in this area

Parenting Area	INITIAL	FINAL	REMARKS
'Good enough' parent			
Setting clear limits			
Play			
Praise			
Tangible rewards			
Looking after ourselves			
Home – school relations			
Attending child's events & Functions			
Extra-curricular clubs for children			
Family Traditions*			
Involving children in house chores			
Social networks			
How well you know your children's friends			
What you do to relax / Your Self Care			
Staying calm and managing anger			
Ignoring annoying behaviours			
Health of Adult Relationships in our Family			

*Family traditions – these are those you do as your family, not your tribe or your community

EVALUATION FORMS

Use the Self Assessment Form at the start and end of the programme to assess the Parent's Learning Journey.

Registered Office: Regal Community Centre, Ridgefield Road, Oxford, OX4 3BY
Colchester Office; Winsley's House, High Street, CO1 1UG
www.afiuk.org ; Tel Tel: 07921 462949 / 07539455974

info@afiuk.org ; @AfricansinUK

CROSS-CULTURAL PARENTING PROGRAM - WHOLE PROGRAMME FINAL EVALUATION

Please complete the provided program evaluation sheet.

We appreciate your comments and suggestions as they will help us to make changes in order to improve the program to meet the needs of other migrant parents.

1. What did you like best about this program?

2. Did you receive information that is helpful to your family?

Yes / No

Please explain

3. What changes would you like to see on the course?

Registered Office: Regal Community Centre, Ridgefield Road, Oxford, OX4 3BY
Colchester Office; Winsley's House, High Street, CO1 1UG
www.afiuk.org ; Tel Tel: 07921 462949 / 07539455974

info@afiuk.org ; @AfricansinUK

4. Was this course:	Were the sessions
too long	too long
too short	too short
just right in length	just right in length

5. What other topics would you like to have discussed related to parenting?

6. Would you recommend this course to others?

Yes / No

7. What do you plan to do to continue getting support for effective parenting?

Registered Office: Regal Community Centre, Ridgefield Road, Oxford, OX4 3BY
Colchester Office; Winsley's House, High Street, CO1 1UG
www.afiuk.org ; Tel Tel: 07921 462949 / 07539455974

info@afiuk.org ; @AfricansinUK

8. Were you happy with the facilities?
9. Were you satisfied with the facilitator?
10. Additional Comments:

Link to the Form : https://forms.gle/7s3g56sedh2JAZNg7

Thank you very much for your time, and Your feedback.

Registered Office: Regal Community Centre, Ridgefield Road, Oxford, OX4 3BY
Colchester Office; Winsley's House, High Street, CO1 1UG
www.afiuk.org ; Tel Tel: 07921 462949 / 07539455974

info@afiuk.org ; @AfricansinUK

CHARTS

AND

ILLUSTRATIONS

Registered Office: Regal Community Centre, Ridgefield Road, Oxford, OX4 3BY
Colchester Office; Winsley's House, High Street, CO1 1UG
www.afiuk.org ; Tel Tel: 07921 462949 / 07539455974

info@afiuk.org ; @AfricansinUK

AFiUK PARENTING BLOCKS

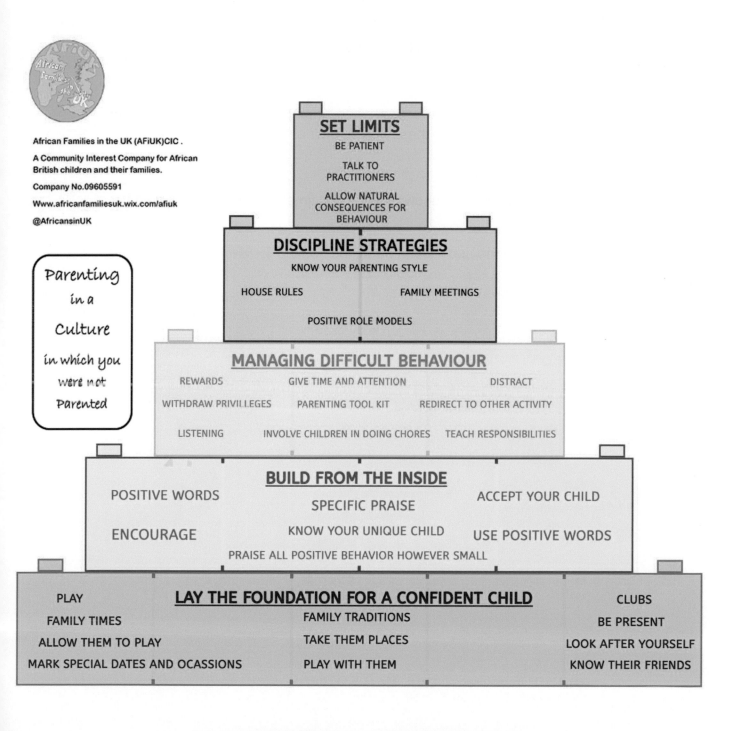

African Families in the UK (AFiUK)CIC .

A Community Interest Company for African British children and their families.

Company No.09605591

Www.africanfamiliesuk.wix.com/afiuk

@AfricansinUK

Parenting in a Culture in which you were not Parented

SET LIMITS
BE PATIENT
TALK TO PRACTITIONERS
ALLOW NATURAL CONSEQUENCES FOR BEHAVIOUR

DISCIPLINE STRATEGIES
KNOW YOUR PARENTING STYLE
HOUSE RULES   FAMILY MEETINGS
POSITIVE ROLE MODELS

MANAGING DIFFICULT BEHAVIOUR
REWARDS   GIVE TIME AND ATTENTION   DISTRACT
WITHDRAW PRIVILLEGES   PARENTING TOOL KIT   REDIRECT TO OTHER ACTIVITY
LISTENING   INVOLVE CHILDREN IN DOING CHORES   TEACH RESPONSIBILITIES

BUILD FROM THE INSIDE
POSITIVE WORDS   SPECIFIC PRAISE   ACCEPT YOUR CHILD
ENCOURAGE   KNOW YOUR UNIQUE CHILD   USE POSITIVE WORDS
PRAISE ALL POSITIVE BEHAVIOR HOWEVER SMALL

LAY THE FOUNDATION FOR A CONFIDENT CHILD
PLAY   FAMILY TRADITIONS   CLUBS
FAMILY TIMES   TAKE THEM PLACES   BE PRESENT
ALLOW THEM TO PLAY   PLAY WITH THEM   LOOK AFTER YOURSELF
MARK SPECIAL DATES AND OCASSIONS   KNOW THEIR FRIENDS

Registered Office: Regal Community Centre, Ridgefield Road, Oxford, OX4 3BY
Colchester Office; Winsley's House, High Street, CO1 1UG
www.afiuk.org ; Tel Tel: 07921 462949 / 07539455974

info@afiuk.org ; @AfricansinUK

PARENTING BLOCKS

Use these blocks to explain to parents the various factors that go into creating positive parenting relationship with ttheir children.

Alll these are covered in our full parenting course

It is a useful tool to use to provide overview when helping parents understand what areas need address and the impact these has on their children.

The size of the building block also shows how much time and resources should be spent on each area,

It also shows how much time and resources will be needed for each area to ensure healthy family relationships.

Registered Office: Regal Community Centre, Ridgefield Road, Oxford, OX4 3BY
Colchester Office; Winsley's House, High Street, CO1 1UG
www.afiuk.org ; Tel Tel: 07921 462949 / 07539455974

info@afiuk.org ; @AfricansinUK

THE PARENTING TRIANGLE

ADULT

- Have Regular Honest reflections about yourself.
- What is going on for you as the adult?
- What are the issues you are dealing with?

Learn to

A C T

not REACT

CHILD

- What does your child Need?
- What is going on for your child?

TOOLS

What tools do you have?
- What tool can you use to make the situaiton better?

www/afiuk.org / info@afiuk.org / 07921 462949

Made with PosterMyWall.com

Registered Office: Regal Community Centre, Ridgefield Road, Oxford, OX4 3BY
Colchester Office; Winsley's House, High Street, CO1 1UG
www.afiuk.org ; Tel Tel: 07921 462949 / 07539455974

info@afiuk.org ; @AfricansinUK

USING THE PARENTING TRIANGLE

We have developed the model of the Parenting Triangle to illustrate the parenting relationship between parents and their children and the tools that they use to keep this relationship healthy.

The triangle is colour coded emulating the traffic lights systems.

-       **RED is for Adults** – Take charge, you are responsible for what happens in this relationships. Stop, Be Alert. Regularly self reflect and deal with any issues that are impacting on your parenting capacity.

-       **Amber is for the Child**.

Children are still growing and developing, their needs change with their age and stage of development.

Children are still learning to self regulate and manage their feelings, needs and behaviour.

Childhood is transcient, and children do not have the luxury of time, so their needs are more immediate and need to be addressed as soon as possible.

-       **Green is for Tools**. Good enough parenting is about the application of the right tools appropriately to keep the relationship progressing well.

This triangle reflects healthy parent-child relationship which is well balanced, (equilateral) – not too skewed on one side.

Not focussing too much on parents' needs or interests only (authoritarian);

not skewed too much on children's wants and interests (permissive, indulgent) ;

not skewed too much on tools and performance (regimental, authoritarian)

This triangle is a useful tool to aid parents' self reflection

Registered Office: Regal Community Centre, Ridgefield Road, Oxford, OX4 3BY
Colchester Office; Winsley's House, High Street, CO1 1UG
www.afiuk.org ; Tel Tel: 07921 462949 / 07539455974

info@afiuk.org ; @AfricansinUK

THE TOOLBOX CONCEPT

AFIUK

The role of parenting requires a skill set which the BOMA programme will equip the parents with;as well as support the parents to use the tools they already have effectively.This programme is not asserting that parents don't know how to parent,BOMA programme recognises that as migrant parents we are combining different cultural,geographical, political and social systems in our family lives.Various trades and activities, such as chef, hair dresser, builders, all require their toolbox for them to do their job well.
So as a parent, what is in your toolbox?

This programme is an opportunity to adapt, add or relinquish some tools.

Registered Office: Regal Community Centre, Ridgefield Road, Oxford, OX4 3BY
Colchester Office; Winsley's House, High Street, CO1 1UG
www.afiuk.org ; Tel Tel: 07921 462949 / 07539455974

info@afiuk.org ; @AfricansinUK

Registered Office: Regal Community Centre, Ridgefield Road, Oxford, OX4 3BY
Colchester Office; Winsley's House, High Street, CO1 1UG
www.afiuk.org ; Tel Tel: 07921 462949 / 07539455974

info@afiuk.org ; @AfricansinUK

60

FEELINGS AND NEEDS FOUNTAIN

It is very easy to notice children's behaviour and begin working very hard to correct the behaviour. However, it is more effective is to seek to understand that all behaviour is communication, and children are expressing a feeling through their behaviour.

Registered Office: Regal Community Centre, Ridgefield Road, Oxford, OX4 3BY
Colchester Office; Winsley's House, High Street, CO1 1UG
www.afiuk.org ; Tel Tel: 07921 462949 / 07539455974

info@afiuk.org ; @AfricansinUK

To even more effectively understand our children's behaviour we need to understand that underneath all the feelings are needs.

Whether needs are met or unmet impacts how children feel and feelings drive their behaviour.

When needs are met, then feelings are positive and fulfilling and the observed behaviour is positive and acceptable.

Positive parenting should aim to meet our children's needs rather than just demand positive behaviour from them.

As children grow older they rely on parents less and less to meet their needs as they begin to learn strategies of meeting their own needs and therefore begin regulating their own behaviour

Familiarise yourself to name feelings and to help your child to name their feelings.

<u>REMEMBER</u>

- **All behaviour is communication**

- **Aim to meet the NEEDS, and then positive FEELINGS and BEHAVIOUR will follow - (make this your main goal,**

Registered Office: Regal Community Centre, Ridgefield Road, Oxford, OX4 3BY
Colchester Office; Winsley's House, High Street, CO1 1UG
www.afiuk.org ; Tel Tel: 07921 462949 / 07539455974

info@afiuk.org ; @AfricansinUK

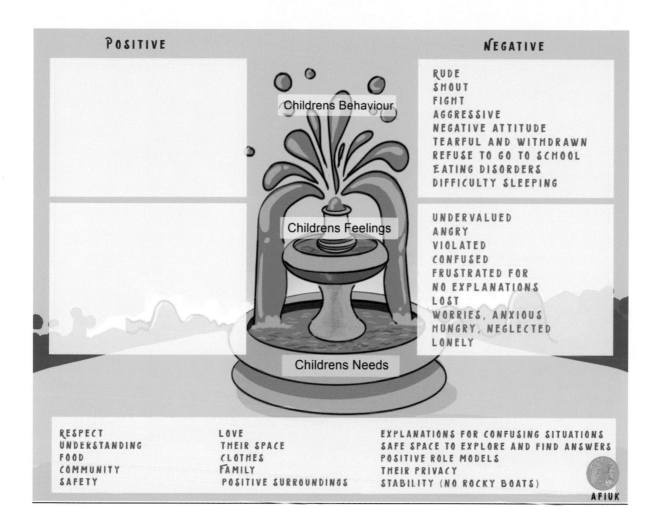

Practice exploring the link between what your child's behaviour may be telling you.

For example, It may be as simple as
Behaviour : a child may be crying,
Feeling : because they are hungry and they
Need : food

Of a child may be
Behaviour : running away from home; or going missing
Feeling : because they feel isolated, confused or worried
Need : explanations or a safe space to explore confusing situations.

Registered Office: Regal Community Centre, Ridgefield Road, Oxford, OX4 3BY
Colchester Office; Winsley's House, High Street, CO1 1UG
www.afiuk.org ; Tel Tel: 07921 462949 / 07539455974

info@afiuk.org ; @AfricansinUK

Parenting In A Culture In Which You Were Not Parented In Yourself.

Registered Office: Regal Community Centre, Ridgefield Road, Oxford, OX4 3BY
Colchester Office; Winsley's House, High Street, CO1 1UG
www.afiuk.org ; Tel Tel: 07921 462949 / 07539455974

info@afiuk.org ; @AfricansinUK

Use the traffic light system to remind you how to deal with problems.

---

1. Listen to your <u>child, and</u> aim to understand their needs.
2. Remember the traffic light symbols, green will always let you go.
3. When you use your tools properly, it keeps the traffic flowing.

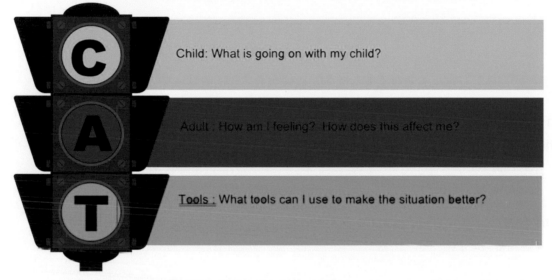

Child: What is going on with my child?

Adult : How am I feeling? How does this affect me?

<u>Tools :</u> What tools can I use to make the situation better?

4. When the child is pushing the boundaries, and you need to maintain the routine, then as a parent you need to **ACT**
5. Remember the traffic light symbols, adult always be alert but calm

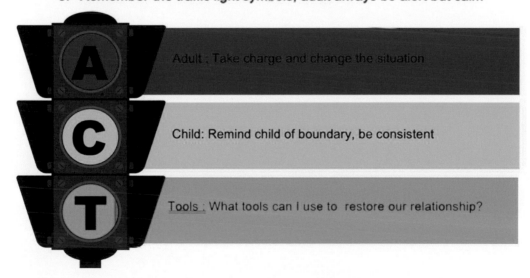

Adult : Take charge and change the situation

Child: Remind child of boundary, be consistent

<u>Tools :</u> What tools can I use to restore our relationship?

Registered Office: Regal Community Centre, Ridgefield Road, Oxford, OX4 3BY
Colchester Office; Winsley's House, High Street, CO1 1UG
www.afiuk.org ; Tel Tel: 07921 462949 / 07539455974

info@afiuk.org ; @AfricansinUK

<u>3 STEPS FOR DEALING WITH AN ANGRY CHILD</u>

ACT! DO NOT RE-ACT

Adult: STOP! Remain calm – Reflect: What is going on for me?

Child: THINK! What does my child need?

Tools: What tool can I use to make the situation better?

As an adult, you need to remain authoritative, do not lose control of the situation by reacting to the situation.

Use this traffic light to illustrate session 6

Registered Office: Regal Community Centre, Ridgefield Road, Oxford, OX4 3BY
Colchester Office; Winsley's House, High Street, CO1 1UG
www.afiuk.org ; Tel Tel: 07921 462949 / 07539455974

info@afiuk.org ; @AfricansinUK

Icebreaker;

coaching parents to be aware of their feelings, what is triggering those feelings and how this could impact their parenting capacity.

- How are you feeling today?

- Write some of the reasons for your temperature then stick it on the thermometer.

Also,

Use this thermometer activity in the Dealing with Anger Activity in Session 5

Parents reflect on their responses to the various scenairos.

I feel fine and in full control of the situation.

I feel fine, but I have some concerns.

I am worried now,

I am very stressed, I need help

Registered Office: Regal Community Centre, Ridgefield Road, Oxford, OX4 3BY
Colchester Office; Winsley's House, High Street, CO1 1UG
www.afiuk.org ; Tel Tel: 07921 462949 / 07539455974

info@afiuk.org ; @AfricansinUK

Registered Office: Regal Community Centre, Ridgefield Road, Oxford, OX4 3BY
Colchester Office; Winsley's House, High Street, CO1 1UG
www.afiuk.org ; Tel Tel: 07921 462949 / 07539455974

info@afiuk.org ; @AfricansinUK

68

SUPPORTED BY

COMMUNITY GRANT

Printed in the United States
by Baker & Taylor Publisher Services